COMMUNICATION
Skills
FOR INSURANCE ADJUSTERS

**MAXIMIZING YOUR VALUE
TO INSURANCE COMPANIES WHILE
PRIORITIZING SELF-CARE**

EFFICIENT ADJUSTER

Communication Skills for Insurance Adjusters: Maximizing Your Value to Insurance Companies While Prioritizing Self-care Copyright © 2023 by Efficient Adjuster

All rights reserved. This book is fully protected under copyright laws of the United States of America, and all the countries covered by the International Copyright Union. No part of this book may be reproduced or transmitted in any form, whole or part, including professional, amateur, motion picture, recitation, lecturing, public reading, radio broadcasting, television video, or sound taping, all other forms stored in a retrieval system, or transmitted in any form or by any means electronic, mechanical, or other without written permission from the author, except by reviewer, who may quote brief passages in a review.

The uploading, scanning, and distribution of this book via the Internet or via any other means without the permission of the publisher is illegal and punishable by law. Please purchase only authorized electronic editions, and do not participate in or encourage electronic piracy of copyrighted materials.

Visit our website at www.efficientadjuster.com.

Email: contact@efficientadjuster.com

Printed in the United States of America

ISBN: 9798373081443

Publisher: Efficient Adjuster

"THE POWER OF COMMUNICATION"

The power of communication,
A force that can't be beat,
It brings us closer together,
And helps us communicate.

With words, we can express,
Our thoughts and feelings deep,
We can solve problems and conflicts,
And our relationships, we can keep.

So let us speak with kindness,
And listen with an open heart,
For when we communicate effectively,
Our connections, they will start.

~ Unknown

CONTENTS

Preface 08

Introduction 12

Chapter 1
The Importance of Communication in Insurance Adjusting 17

Chapter 2
Listening Skills 21

Chapter 3
Verbal Communication 25

Chapter 4
Written Communication 34

Chapter 5
Interpersonal Communication 37

Chapter 6
Conflict Resolution 40

Chapter 7
Developing Your Communication Skills 45

Chapter 8
Emotional Intelligence 49

Chapter 9
Empathy 54

Chapter 10
Time Management 57

Chapter 11
Teamwork 61

Chapter 12
Goals, Deadlines, and Workload 68

Chapter 13
Navigating Legal and Regulatory Issues 74

Chapter 14
Questioning Techniques 77

Chapter 15
Dealing with Difficult Clients and Situations 82

Chapter 16
Self-Care 88

Epilogue 97

PREFACE

A good adjuster is not only knowledgeable about insurance policies and legal procedures, but also possesses a range of soft skills that enable them to effectively communicate with claimants, negotiate with stakeholders, and navigate the often-complex world of insurance claims. These soft skills, also known as interpersonal or people skills, are becoming increasingly important in the modern world of work, where the ability to work well with others and effectively solve problems is highly valued.

In this book, we will explore the various soft skills that are essential for adjusters to succeed in their roles. We will cover topics such as effective communication, empathy, active listening, problem-solving, conflict resolution, and emotional intelligence. Through a combination of theory, real-world examples, and practical exercises, we aim to provide you with the knowledge and tools you need to develop and enhance your own soft skills.

But first, let's take a closer look at what exactly we mean by "soft skills." Unlike hard skills, which refer to specific, technical knowledge or abilities, soft skills are more intangible and related to how we interact with others. They are often described as the "people skills" that are necessary to get along with others, build relationships, and work effectively as part of a team.

Effective communication is one of the most important soft skills for adjusters, as it involves the ability to clearly convey information and ideas to others, as well as listen actively and understand the perspectives of others. This includes both verbal and written communication, and being able to adapt your communication style to different audiences and situations.

Empathy is another essential soft skill for adjusters, as it involves being able to understand and share the feelings of others. This is important in the insurance industry, where adjusters often work with claimants who may be experiencing stress, anxiety, or other strong emotions as a result of an accident or loss. By demonstrating empathy, adjusters can help claimants feel heard and understood, which can go a long way towards building trust and cooperation.

Active listening is closely related to empathy and involves fully focusing on what the other person is saying, rather than just waiting for your turn to speak. This includes paying attention to nonverbal cues, asking clarifying questions, and summarizing what the other person has said to ensure that you have a clear understanding. Active listening is an important skill for adjusters, as it enables them to accurately gather information and build rapport with claimants.

Problem-solving is another key soft skill for adjusters, as they often need to identify and resolve complex issues in order to come to a fair and satisfactory resolution for all parties involved. This involves being able to analyze problems, think critically, and come up with creative solutions.

Conflict resolution is another important soft skill for adjusters, as conflicts and disputes can arise in the course of an insurance claim. This involves being able to effectively manage and resolve conflicts in a way that is fair and respectful to all parties involved.

Emotional intelligence is another crucial soft skill for adjusters, as it involves being aware of and managing your own emotions, as well as being able to understand and respond appropriately to the emotions of others. This includes being able to regulate your own emotions, as well as being able to recognize and respond to the emotions of others in a way that is supportive and constructive.

As an insurance adjuster, effective communication is a vital aspect of your job. Your ability to effectively communicate with policyholders, claimants, and colleagues can greatly impact your value to insurance companies. Not only that, but it is important to prioritize self-care in order to maintain your own well-being while navigating the often-stressful world of insurance.

Adjusters are constantly interacting with individuals who are often dealing with difficult situations. This may include policyholders who have experienced loss or damage to their property, or claimants who have experienced injury or illness. It is your job to communicate with these individuals in a compassionate and understanding manner, while also being firm and decisive when necessary. You must also be able to effectively communicate with your colleagues. This may include working with other adjusters to assess and evaluate claims, as well as communicating with supervisors and management to report on the progress of your cases. Clear and concise communication is key in order to ensure that all parties involved are on the same page and working towards the same goals.

While it is important to prioritize your communication skills in order to maximize your value to insurance companies, it is equally important to prioritize self-care. The insurance industry can be a fast-paced and high-stress environment, and it is essential to take care of yourself in order to avoid burnout. This may include setting boundaries, taking breaks, and finding healthy ways to cope with stress.

In this book, we will delve into each of these soft skills in more detail, providing you with the knowledge and tools you need to develop and enhance your own skills in these areas. We will also provide real-world examples and practical exercises to help you apply these concepts in your daily work as an adjuster.

Communication skills are a critical aspect of the insurance adjuster role, and it is important to prioritize both your communication skills and your own well-being in order to succeed in this field. By effectively communicating with policyholders, claimants, and colleagues, while also prioritizing self-care, you can maximize your value to insurance companies and maintain a healthy and successful career in the insurance industry.

We hope that this book will serve as a valuable resource for adjusters looking to improve their soft skills. Whether you're looking for a new career in insurance, want to improve your performance or want to be promoted within the company, this book helps both experienced and beginner adjusters to be more successful.

INTRODUCTION

In this book, we will explore the various soft skills that are essential for adjusters to master. These skills include effective communication, active listening, empathy, conflict resolution, time management, and teamwork. We will also discuss how to develop and improve these skills, as well as strategies for applying them in the workplace.

Soft skills are a crucial part of any professional's toolkit, but they are especially important for adjusters. As the people who are responsible for evaluating and settling insurance claims, adjusters must be able to communicate effectively, build relationships with clients, and handle difficult situations with tact and professionalism. In this book, we will explore the various soft skills that are essential for adjusters and provide practical tips for developing and honing these skills.

Effective communication is crucial for adjusters, as you are constantly interacting with clients, colleagues, and other professionals. You need to be able to clearly convey your thoughts and ideas, as well as listen carefully to others in order to fully understand their needs and concerns. We will explore different communication styles and how to adapt your approach to different audiences. This involves not only being able to speak clearly and concisely, but also being able to listen actively and ask the right questions. Adjusters must be able to explain complex concepts in a way that is easy for clients to understand, and they must be able to communicate their findings and recommendations in a way that is clear and persuasive.

Active listening is a key component of effective communication.

It involves paying attention to what others are saying, asking clarifying questions, and showing that you understand their perspective. We will discuss how to hone your active listening skills, including how to avoid distractions and minimize interruptions.

Empathy is the ability to understand and share the feelings of others. As an adjuster, you may be dealing with clients who are upset, anxious, or angry. Having empathy allows you to connect with them on a deeper level and provide the support and guidance they need during a difficult time. We will discuss ways to cultivate empathy, including techniques for putting yourself in others' shoes and showing genuine concern.

Conflict resolution is another important soft skill for adjusters. Disputes and disagreements are a natural part of any work environment, and it is up to you to find ways to resolve them in a fair and amicable manner. We will discuss strategies for handling conflict, including how to stay calm and focused, identify the root causes of a disagreement, and work towards mutually beneficial solutions.

Time management is essential for adjusters, as you often have multiple tasks and deadlines to juggle. We will discuss techniques for prioritizing your workload, setting goals and deadlines, and using tools like calendars and to-do lists to stay organized.

Teamwork is also an important soft skill for adjusters, as you often work with colleagues and other professionals in order to resolve claims and provide the best possible service to clients. We will discuss how to build and maintain positive working relationships, including how to collaborate effectively, offer and accept feedback, and contribute to a positive team culture.

Throughout this book, we will provide practical tips and

exercises to help you develop and improve your soft skills. By mastering these skills, you will be better equipped to handle the challenges of the insurance industry and provide top-notch service to your clients.

Another important soft skill for adjusters is the ability to build relationships with clients. Adjusters must be able to establish trust and rapport with clients, even in difficult or stressful situations. This involves being empathetic and understanding, as well as being able to provide reassurance and support. Adjusters who are able to build strong relationships with their clients are often more successful at settling claims and helping clients navigate the insurance process.

In addition to communication and relationship-building skills, adjusters must also be able to handle difficult situations with tact and professionalism. This includes being able to manage conflict, handle challenging clients, and navigate complex legal and regulatory issues. Adjusters who are able to stay calm and composed under pressure are more likely to be successful in their roles.

To help adjusters develop and hone their soft skills, this book will cover a range of topics, including:

- Active listening and questioning techniques
- Communication strategies for explaining complex concepts
- Building trust and rapport with clients
- Empathy and emotional intelligence
- Conflict resolution and problem-solving
- Dealing with difficult clients and situations
- Navigating legal and regulatory issues

Throughout the book, we will provide practical tips and exercises to help adjusters develop their soft skills and apply them in real-world situations. We will also explore case studies and real-world examples to illustrate the importance of these skills in the insurance industry.

As an insurance adjuster, strong communication skills are essential to your success in the industry. Not only do they allow you to effectively gather and assess information about insurance claims, but they also help you build trust and rapport with clients and colleagues. In this book, we will discuss the importance of communication skills for insurance adjusters and how to maximize your value to insurance companies while prioritizing self-care.

However, it's important to remember that communication skills go beyond just speaking and listening. They also involve being able to understand and empathize with clients and colleagues. This means being able to put yourself in someone else's shoes and show compassion and understanding towards their situation. By being able to connect with clients on a personal level, you can build trust and strengthen your relationships with them.

While effective communication is essential for insurance adjusters, it's also important to prioritize self-care. The demands of the job can be overwhelming at times, and it's important to take breaks and prioritize your own well-being. This may involve setting boundaries with clients and colleagues, taking breaks throughout the day, or seeking support from a mentor or counselor. By taking care of yourself, you can ensure that you have the energy and focus to perform at your best and provide high-quality service to clients.

Whether you are a seasoned adjuster looking to improve your skills or a new adjuster just starting out in your career, this book will provide valuable insights and strategies for developing the soft skills that are essential to success in this field. With the right tools and strategies, you can become a more effective and successful adjuster, able to navigate even the most challenging situations with confidence and professionalism.

Chapter

1

THE IMPORTANCE OF COMMUNICATION IN INSURANCE ADJUSTING

Effective communication is crucial in any profession, but it is especially important in the field of insurance adjusting. Insurance adjusters are responsible for evaluating and settling insurance claims, which often involves interacting with policyholders, claimants, and other stakeholders. In order to effectively assess and resolve claims, adjusters must be able to communicate clearly and effectively with all parties involved.

One of the primary functions of an insurance adjuster is to gather information about a claim. This often involves interviewing policyholders and claimants, as well as reviewing documents and other evidence related to the claim. In order to obtain all of the necessary information, adjusters must be able to communicate effectively with policyholders and claimants, asking the right questions and actively listening to their responses. Adjusters must also be able to explain complex insurance policies and terms in a way that is understandable to those who may not be familiar with insurance terminology.

Effective communication is also important when it comes to negotiating settlements with claimants. Adjusters must be able to clearly present the terms of a settlement offer, as well as explain the reasoning behind the offer. They must also be able to listen to the concerns of claimants and respond to their questions or objections in a way that is fair and respectful.

In addition to interacting with policyholders and claimants, insurance adjusters often work with other stakeholders, including other insurance adjusters, lawyers, and experts in various fields. In order to effectively collaborate with these professionals, adjusters must be able to communicate clearly and concisely, both in writing and in person.

Effective communication is also important when it comes to managing customer expectations. Policyholders and claimants may have certain expectations about the claims process and the resolution of their claim. Adjusters must be able to communicate clearly and honestly about what is covered under a policy and what is not, as well as the timeline for resolving a claim.

Effective communication is a crucial aspect of self-care for adjusters, as it allows them to effectively manage their workload and relationships with clients, colleagues, and superiors. It also plays a key role in reducing stress and promoting overall well-being.

Effective communication involves both verbal and nonverbal communication, and it is important for adjusters to be aware of how they are expressing themselves in order to communicate effectively. Verbal communication includes the words that are spoken, while nonverbal communication includes facial expressions, body language, and tone of voice.

One key aspect of effective communication is being able to listen actively. This involves paying attention to what is being said, asking clarifying questions, and providing feedback. By actively listening, adjusters can better understand the needs and concerns of their clients, colleagues, and superiors, and can respond more effectively to those needs.

Another important aspect of effective communication is the use of assertive language. Assertive language involves expressing oneself clearly and directly, without being aggressive or passive. This can help adjusters to communicate their needs and boundaries effectively, and can help to prevent misunderstandings and conflicts.

Effective communication also involves being aware of cultural differences and being respectful of others' communication styles. This includes understanding the body language, social norms, and cultural values of those with whom you are communicating. By being sensitive to these differences, adjusters can better connect with and understand their clients, colleagues, and superiors.

In addition to verbal and nonverbal communication, effective communication also involves the use of technology. This includes email, phone calls, and videoconferencing, which can all be used to effectively communicate with clients, colleagues, and superiors. It is important for adjusters to be aware of the appropriate use of technology for different situations, and to be mindful of the potential for misunderstandings when communicating through technology.

Effective communication is a key aspect of self-care for

adjusters, as it allows them to effectively manage their workload and relationships, and promotes overall well-being. By being aware of their own communication style, actively listening, using assertive language, being sensitive to cultural differences, and using technology appropriately, adjusters can effectively communicate with clients, colleagues, and superiors, and better manage the demands of their work.

In summary, effective communication is essential for insurance adjusters in order to gather necessary information, negotiate settlements, collaborate with other professionals, and manage customer expectations. Strong communication skills can help adjusters resolve claims efficiently and fairly, leading to better outcomes for policyholders and claimants.

Chapter 2

LISTENING SKILLS

Effective listening is an important skill for adjusters to develop, as it allows them to accurately gather information from clients, witnesses, and other parties involved in a claim. There are several theories and practical applications of effective listening that can help adjusters improve their skills in this area.

One theory of effective listening is called the "four-ear model," developed by Michael D. Krass. This model suggests that there are four different ways in which we can listen: passively, actively, critically, and empathetically.

Passive listening involves simply hearing the words being spoken without really engaging with the content. This type of listening is often seen as the least effective, as it does not allow the listener to fully understand the speaker's perspective or needs.

Active listening, on the other hand, involves actively engaging with the content of the conversation and showing the speaker that you are paying attention. This can be done through nonverbal cues such as nodding or maintaining eye contact, as well as through verbal cues such as repeating back key points or asking clarifying questions. Active listening helps to build trust and rapport between the listener and the speaker, and can be particularly useful for adjusters when working with clients who may be upset or distressed.

Critical listening involves evaluating the content of the conversation and considering whether it is accurate or relevant. This type of listening is important for adjusters as it helps them to assess the validity of a claim and determine the appropriate course of action.

Empathetic listening involves attempting to understand and feel the emotions of the speaker. This type of listening is important for adjusters as it allows them to show the speaker that they are being heard and understood, and can help to build trust and rapport.

In addition to these theories of effective listening, there are several practical techniques that adjusters can use to improve their listening skills. These include:

1. Avoiding distractions: It is important for adjusters to minimize distractions when listening to clients or other parties involved in a claim. This might involve finding a quiet, private place to conduct the conversation, or turning off electronic devices.

2. Paying attention: Adjusters should focus their attention on the speaker and avoid multitasking or thinking about other things while listening.

3. Using nonverbal cues: Nonverbal cues such as eye contact,

nodding, and facial expressions can help to show the speaker that you are engaged in the conversation and interested in what they have to say.

4. Asking clarifying questions: Asking questions can help to clarify any misunderstandings or confusion, and can also show the speaker that you are interested in what they have to say.

5. Paraphrasing: Repeating back key points or paraphrasing what the speaker has said can help to ensure that you have understood the content of the conversation.

Overall, effective listening is an important skill for adjusters to develop, as it allows them to accurately gather information and build trust with clients and other parties involved in a claim. By using theories such as the four-ear model and practical techniques like avoiding distractions and asking clarifying questions, adjusters can improve their listening skills and better serve the needs of their clients.

As an adjuster, it is important to take care of yourself in order to effectively handle the demands of your job. One important aspect of self-care is developing strong listening skills.

Listening is often overlooked as a form of self-care, but it is crucial for maintaining healthy relationships, increasing productivity, and reducing stress. When we actively listen to others, we show that we value their thoughts and feelings, which can improve communication and build trust. Additionally, listening allows us to better understand and solve problems, leading to increased efficiency and reduced frustration. skills as an adjuster. First, it is important to focus your attention on the person speaking. This means putting away distractions like your phone or laptop and giving the speaker your full attention. It is also helpful to make eye contact and nod or give other nonverbal cues to show that you are engaged in the conversation.

Another key to effective listening is being present in the moment. This means setting aside your own thoughts and biases and truly trying to understand the perspective of the person speaking. It can be helpful to repeat back what you heard to ensure that you accurately understood their message.

In addition to these strategies, it is important to remain open-minded and nonjudgmental when listening. This means being willing to consider different viewpoints and not making assumptions about the speaker based on your own beliefs or experiences.

Developing strong listening skills can also have positive impacts on your personal relationships. By actively listening to your loved ones, you can build stronger connections and show that you value their thoughts and feelings.

In the fast-paced world of adjusting, it can be tempting to rush through conversations and make assumptions about what others are saying. However, taking the time to truly listen can not only improve your work performance, but also benefit your personal relationships and overall well-being. By incorporating listening as a form of self-care, you can better handle the demands of your job and lead a happier, healthier life.

Chapter 3

VERBAL COMMUNICATION AND NON-VERBAL COMMUNICATION

Effective listening skills are crucial for adjusters, as they often deal with complex and sensitive situations that require a high degree of empathy and understanding. In this chapter, we will discuss both verbal and non-verbal communication, and provide some theories and practical tips on how to hone your listening skills.

Verbal Communication

Verbal communication refers to the words that are used to convey a message. There are several theories and models that can help adjusters improve their verbal listening skills.

One such model is the S-R-E Model, which stands for Stimulus, Response, and Evaluation. This model suggests that effective listening involves three steps:

1. Stimulus: The speaker provides a stimulus (i.e., a message) that is intended to elicit a response from the listener.

2. Response: The listener responds to the stimulus by providing feedback, asking questions, or expressing understanding.

3. Evaluation: The listener evaluates the stimulus by considering the content, context, and tone of the message, and determining its relevance and importance.

Another theory is the Hierarchy of Listening, which proposes that there are different levels of listening, each requiring a different level of effort and attention. The levels are:

1. Level 1: Passive listening – This is when the listener is not actively engaged in the conversation and is simply letting the words wash over them.

2. Level 2: Selective listening – This is when the listener is selectively paying attention to certain parts of the conversation and ignoring others.

3. Level 3: Active listening – This is when the listener is fully engaged in the conversation, focusing on the words, tone, and body language of the speaker, and providing feedback and clarification when necessary.

4. Level 4: Empathetic listening – This is when the listener not only understands the words and feelings of the speaker, but also tries to put themselves in the speaker's shoes and feel what they are feeling.

To be an effective listener, it is important to strive for level 3 and 4 listening, as these require the most effort and attention, but also provide the greatest benefits. Some practical tips for achieving these levels of listening include:

- Maintain eye contact: This helps to show the speaker that you are paying attention and interested in what they have to say.

- Avoid distractions: Turn off your phone, close your laptop, and eliminate any other distractions that might prevent you from fully focusing on the conversation.

- Clarify and confirm: If you are not sure you understood something, don't be afraid to ask for clarification or confirmation. This helps to ensure that you have a clear understanding of the message.

- Reflect and summarize: Repeat back to the speaker what you heard, in your own words, to show that you were paying attention and understood their message.

Some key non-verbal cues to look for include:

- Eye contact: As mentioned above, maintaining eye contact can show that you are engaged and interested in the conversation. Conversely, avoiding eye contact can indicate disinterest or dishonesty.

- Facial expressions: Smiling, frowning, raising eyebrows, and other facial expressions can convey a wide range of emotions, and can help you understand how the speaker is feeling.

- Gestures: Hand gestures, head nods, and other body

movements can help to convey meaning and emphasis, and can provide valuable context.

Effective listening skills are crucial for adjusters, as they must be able to accurately gather and interpret information from clients and colleagues in order to make informed decisions. There are several theories and practical applications that can help adjusters improve their listening skills, including the importance of non-verbal communication.

Non-verbal communication includes body language, facial expressions, and tone of voice, all of which can provide important clues about the speaker's true intentions and emotions. For example, if a client is visibly upset or frustrated, their non-verbal cues may be more informative than their words in determining the root cause of their dissatisfaction. Adjusters should be attuned to these non-verbal cues and use them to better understand the speaker's perspective.

In addition to active listening and paying attention to non-verbal communication, adjusters can also improve their listening skills by being mindful of their own biases and preconceptions. It is easy to let our own beliefs and assumptions influence our interpretation of what we hear, but this can lead to misunderstandings and even conflict. By being aware of our own biases and attempting to remain open-minded, adjusters can better understand the perspectives of others and make more informed decisions.

One practical application of effective listening skills for adjusters is the use of reflective listening. Reflective listening involves restating or paraphrasing what the speaker has said, in order to show that you have fully understood their message and to give them the opportunity to clarify any misunderstandings. This can be especially helpful in situations where the speaker may be upset or emotional, as it allows them to feel heard and understood.

Another practical application of effective listening skills for adjusters is the use of empathetic listening. Empathetic listening involves not only understanding the words the speaker is saying, but also trying to put yourself in their shoes and understand their perspective. This can be especially important in situations where the speaker may be angry or upset, as it allows the adjuster to approach the situation with compassion and understanding rather than defensiveness.

Overall, effective listening skills are crucial for adjusters in order to accurately gather and interpret information, make informed decisions, and build trust and rapport with clients and colleagues. By being attuned to non-verbal communication, being mindful of biases, and using reflective and empathetic listening techniques, adjusters can improve their listening skills and better serve their clients.

Verbal and nonverbal communication are two forms of communication that we use on a daily basis. They are both important tools in expressing ourselves and interacting with others. As adjusters, it is crucial to have effective communication skills in order to effectively communicate with clients and colleagues. However, it is also important to practice self-care when it comes to communication, as it can be emotionally and mentally draining to constantly communicate with others.

Verbal communication refers to the use of words and language to express oneself. This includes speaking, writing, and even sign language. Verbal communication is essential in conveying information, but it is also important to pay attention to the tone and delivery of the message. The way we say something can have a huge impact on how it is received by others.

Nonverbal communication refers to the use of body language, gestures, and facial expressions to convey meaning. Nonverbal communication can often be more powerful than verbal communication, as it allows us to express emotions and convey unspoken messages. However, nonverbal communication can also be misleading, as it is often culturally specific and can be misinterpreted.

As adjusters, it is important to pay attention to both verbal and nonverbal communication in order to effectively communicate with clients and colleagues. It is also important to practice self-care when it comes to communication. Here are a few ways to take care of yourself through verbal and nonverbal communication:

1. Set boundaries: It is important to set boundaries when it comes to communication, especially if you are dealing with high-stress or emotional situations. It is okay to take a break and step away from the conversation if you need to.

2. Practice active listening: Active listening involves paying attention to what the other person is saying, not just waiting for your turn to speak. This allows for better understanding and can help to deescalate a situation.

3. Use positive language: Instead of using negative or confrontational language, try to use positive language to communicate your thoughts and feelings. This can help to defuse a situation and foster a more positive relationship.

4. Be aware of your body language: Your body language can speak louder than words. Be aware of your posture, facial expressions, and gestures, and try to use them to convey your message effectively.

5. Take breaks: Communication can be draining, especially in high-stress situations. Take breaks to recharge and practice self-care. This can help you to be more effective in your communication.

Verbal and nonverbal communication are essential tools for adjusters to effectively communicate with clients and colleagues. However, it is also important to practice self-care when it comes to communication, by setting boundaries, practicing active listening, using positive language, being aware of your body language, and taking breaks as needed. By taking care of yourself through communication, you can be more effective and better able to handle the demands of your job as an adjuster.

Professionalism and verbal and nonverbal communication

Verbal and nonverbal communication are crucial elements of professionalism for adjusters. Both forms of communication play a significant role in how adjusters interact with clients, colleagues, and other stakeholders. In this section, we will explore the importance of verbal and nonverbal communication in the field of adjusting, and how professionals can effectively utilize these skills to convey information, build relationships, and resolve conflicts.

Verbal communication refers to the use of spoken language to convey information, ideas, and emotions. It is an essential aspect of professionalism for adjusters because it allows them to explain complex concepts and processes to clients, colleagues, and other stakeholders. Effective verbal communication also involves listening and responding to others, which helps to build trust and establish rapport.

Nonverbal communication, on the other hand, refers to the use of body language, gestures, and facial expressions to convey meaning. It is an important aspect of professionalism for adjusters because it can help to enhance the effectiveness of verbal communication and provide additional context or meaning to a message. For example, nonverbal cues such as eye contact, facial expressions, and posture can all convey confidence, empathy, or aggression.

One of the key challenges that adjusters face when it comes to verbal and nonverbal communication is the fact that these forms of communication are often unconscious and automatic. As a result, adjusters may not be aware of how their words or body language are being perceived by others. This can lead to misunderstandings and conflicts, which can have a negative impact on professionalism.

To address this challenge, adjusters need to be aware of their own verbal and nonverbal communication habits and strive to communicate in a way that is clear, respectful, and effective. This may involve practicing active listening, using positive body language, and avoiding jargon or technical language that may be confusing to clients.

Another important aspect of professionalism for adjusters is the ability to adapt their communication style to different situations and audiences. This may involve using more formal language and body language in formal settings, or adopting a more casual and friendly tone in informal settings. Adjusters should also be aware of cultural differences in communication styles and make an effort to be sensitive to the needs and preferences of their clients and colleagues.

In conclusion, verbal and nonverbal communication are critical elements of professionalism for adjusters. By using these skills effectively, adjusters can successfully convey information, build relationships, and resolve conflicts. Adjusters who are aware of their own communication habits and are able to adapt their style to different situations and audiences will be better equipped to succeed in their roles as professionals.

Chapter 4

WRITTEN COMMUNICATION

Effective written communication skills are essential for adjusters in order to accurately convey information and effectively communicate with clients, colleagues, and other stakeholders. The ability to write clearly, concisely, and persuasively can greatly improve an adjuster's ability to persuade clients and negotiate settlements.

There are several theories that can help adjusters improve their written communication skills. One theory is the rhetorical triangle, which consists of three elements: the speaker, the audience, and the purpose. The speaker is the person communicating the message, the audience is the person or group receiving the message, and the purpose is the goal of the message. Understanding the rhetorical triangle can help adjusters tailor their written communication to their audience and purpose.

Another theory is the cognitive-relational theory, which posits that effective communication relies on the sender's ability to create a shared understanding with the receiver. This involves using language that the receiver can understand, being clear and concise, and using examples and analogies to explain complex concepts. Adjusters should also consider the receiver's perspective and try to anticipate any misunderstandings or concerns they may have.

Practical applications of these theories can help adjusters improve their written communication skills. One key aspect is organization. Adjusters should clearly outline the main points they want to convey and present them in a logical order. They should also use headings and bullet points to break up the text and make it easier to read.

Adjusters should also focus on clarity and conciseness. They should avoid using jargon or complex language that may be difficult for the reader to understand. Instead, they should use simple, straightforward language and explain any technical terms or concepts as needed.

In addition, adjusters should use active voice whenever possible. This means that the subject of the sentence is doing the action, rather than the action being done to the subject. For example, "The adjuster reviewed the claim" is in active voice, while "The claim was reviewed by the adjuster" is in passive voice. Using active voice makes the writing more direct and engages the reader more effectively.

Adjusters should also consider the tone of their written communication. The tone should be professional and respectful, but not overly formal. Adjusters should aim to build a rapport with their readers and create a sense of trust.

Another important aspect of effective written communication

for adjusters is the use of evidence to support their claims. This can include statistics, case studies, expert opinions, and other forms of evidence. Adjusters should be careful to use credible sources and present the evidence in a clear and concise manner.

Adjusters should also be aware of their audience's needs and expectations. This may involve adapting the language and tone of their writing to suit the audience, or including additional information or resources to address any specific concerns or questions the audience may have.

Finally, adjusters should always proofread their written communication for spelling, grammar, and punctuation errors. These errors can undermine the credibility and effectiveness of the message and create confusion for the reader.

In summary, effective written communication skills are crucial for adjusters in order to effectively convey information and persuade clients. Understanding theories such as the rhetorical triangle and cognitive-relational theory can help adjusters tailor their writing to their audience and purpose. Practical applications, such as clear organization, conciseness, active voice, and appropriate tone, can also help adjusters improve their written communication skills. Additionally, the use of evidence and consideration of the audience's needs and expectations can enhance the effectiveness of written communication. Finally, careful proofreading is essential to ensure that written communication is error-free and credible.

Chapter 5

INTERPERSONAL COMMUNICATION

Interpersonal communication skills are essential for adjusters in order to effectively handle claims, negotiate settlements, and build relationships with clients. However, there are some unusual skills that can help adjusters stand out and excel in their field. These skills include active listening, empathy, assertiveness, and emotional intelligence.

Active listening is the practice of fully paying attention to the person speaking and actively trying to understand their perspective. This involves not just hearing the words being spoken, but also understanding the underlying emotions and meanings behind them. For adjusters, active listening can be especially useful when dealing with clients who are upset or distressed about their loss. By actively listening and showing genuine concern, adjusters can build trust and establish a more positive relationship with the client.

Empathy is the ability to understand and share the feelings

of others. This skill is important for adjusters because it allows them to connect with clients on a deeper level and show that they genuinely care about their well-being. Empathy can also help adjusters to better understand the perspective of clients and negotiate settlements that are fair and reasonable for both parties.

Assertiveness is the ability to communicate effectively and stand up for oneself in a respectful and confident manner. This skill is important for adjusters because it allows them to effectively advocate for their clients and negotiate fair settlements without being aggressive or confrontational. Assertiveness also helps adjusters to set boundaries and communicate their needs and expectations clearly and effectively.

Emotional intelligence is the ability to recognize and manage one's own emotions, as well as the emotions of others. This skill is important for adjusters because it allows them to better understand the emotional state of their clients and to communicate with them in a way that is sensitive and appropriate. Emotional intelligence can also help adjusters to handle difficult situations and conflicts more effectively, more on Emotional Intelligence in chapter eight.

There are several theories and practical applications of these interpersonal communication skills in the field of insurance adjusting. One theory is the social exchange theory, which suggests that people engage in communication in order to achieve a desired outcome. In the context of insurance adjusting, this could mean that adjusters use their communication skills to build trust and rapport with clients in order to reach a mutually beneficial settlement.

Another theory is the social learning theory, which suggests that people learn communication skills through observation and imitation. For adjusters, this means that they can learn and develop their communication skills by observing and imitating the behavior of successful colleagues and mentors.

Practical applications of these skills in the field of insurance adjusting include using active listening to fully understand the needs and concerns of clients, using empathy to connect with clients on a deeper level and show genuine concern for their wellbeing, using assertiveness to advocate for clients and negotiate fair settlements, and using emotional intelligence to understand and manage the emotions of clients and handle difficult situations effectively.

In conclusion, unusual interpersonal communication skills such as active listening, empathy, assertiveness, and emotional intelligence are essential for insurance adjusters in order to effectively handle claims, negotiate settlements, and build relationships with clients. These skills can be learned and developed through theories such as the social exchange theory and the social learning theory, and they can be applied in practical ways in the field of insurance adjusting. By mastering these skills, adjusters can stand out and excel in their field, and they can better serve the needs of their clients.

Chapter 6

CONFLICT RESOLUTION AND PROBLEM-SOLVING

Conflict resolution is an essential skill for adjusters, as they often work with clients who may be dealing with difficult and emotional situations. Adjusters must be able to effectively communicate with clients, understand their needs and concerns, and work with them to resolve conflicts and find solutions to problems. In this chapter, we will discuss some theories and practical applications of conflict resolution and problem solving that can help adjusters navigate challenging situations and achieve successful outcomes.

One of the key theories of conflict resolution is the Thomas-Kilmann Conflict Mode Instrument (TKI). Developed by Kenneth Thomas and Ralph Kilmann in the 1970s, the TKI is a tool that helps individuals understand how they tend to approach conflicts and identify strategies that may be more effective in resolving them. According to the TKI, there are five main modes of conflict resolution: competing, collaborating, compromising, avoiding, and accommodating.

Competing involves trying to win or get what you want at the expense of others. This mode may be appropriate in situations where there is a clear winner and loser, such as in a negotiation or a sporting event. However, it is generally not a good strategy for long-term relationships or for resolving conflicts in a cooperative manner.

Collaborating involves working together to find a win-win solution that meets the needs and concerns of all parties involved. This mode is often the most effective for resolving conflicts, as it requires open and honest communication and a willingness to listen to and understand others' perspectives.

Compromising involves finding a middle ground or a solution that meets the needs of all parties to some extent, but may not fully satisfy anyone. This mode may be appropriate in situations where a win-win solution is not possible, or where time is of the essence.

Avoiding involves avoiding the conflict altogether or putting it off for another time. This mode may be appropriate in situations where the conflict is not particularly important or where there is a more pressing issue to deal with. However, if the conflict is not addressed, it may fester and become a bigger problem in the future.

Accommodating involves putting the needs and concerns of others ahead of your own. This mode may be appropriate in situations where the relationship or the greater good is more important than winning the conflict. However, if it is used too often, it may lead to resentment and a feeling of being taken advantage of.

In practice, adjusters may use a combination of these modes

to resolve conflicts, depending on the specific situation and the needs of the parties involved. For example, an adjuster may start by collaborating with a client to find a mutually beneficial solution, but if that is not possible, they may consider compromising or accommodating to find a resolution.

One of the key skills for effective conflict resolution is effective communication. This involves being able to listen actively and attentively, express your own needs and concerns clearly and respectfully, and seek to understand the perspectives of others. Communication is also about being able to manage emotions and maintain a positive and respectful tone, even when dealing with difficult or emotional situations.

Effective communication also involves being able to use effective questioning techniques to gather information and clarify misunderstandings. This includes using open-ended questions, which invite the other person to provide more information or explain their perspective, and using closed-ended questions, which are more specific and require a yes or no answer. By using both types of questions, adjusters can better understand the needs and concerns of their clients and identify potential solutions.

Another important aspect of conflict resolution is problem solving. This involves identifying the underlying causes of the conflict, brainstorming potential solutions, evaluating the pros and cons of each option, and selecting the most appropriate solution.

Problem solving is an essential skill for adjusters, as they are constantly faced with complex issues that require creative and effective solutions. There are a variety of approaches to problem solving, each with its own set of theories and practical applications. In this chapter, we will explore several different approaches to problem solving, including linear, non-linear, and heuristic approaches, as well as the role of creativity and collaboration in effective problem solving.

Linear approaches to problem solving involve breaking a problem down into smaller, more manageable pieces and addressing each piece separately. This approach is often used in scientific and mathematical problem solving, where the problem can be broken down into a series of steps or equations that lead to a clear solution. One example of a linear approach to problem solving is the scientific method, which involves identifying a problem, developing a hypothesis, collecting data, analyzing the data, and reaching a conclusion. This approach is often seen as systematic and logical, and is well suited to problems with clear, objective solutions.

However, not all problems can be solved using a linear approach. Non-linear approaches to problem solving involve more flexible, open-ended approaches that are well suited to complex, dynamic problems. These approaches often involve exploring multiple options and approaches, and may involve trial and error, experimentation, and collaboration with others. Non-linear approaches to problem solving may include brainstorming, mind mapping, and lateral thinking, all of which involve generating a wide range of ideas and options rather than focusing on a single, predetermined solution.

Heuristic approaches to problem solving involve using shortcuts or rules of thumb to guide decision making. These approaches can be useful when faced with complex, unfamiliar problems, as they provide a framework for making decisions and taking action. Examples of heuristic approaches to problem solving include the 80/20 rule, which suggests that 80% of results come from 20% of causes, and the rule of three, which suggests that the best solution is often found by considering the first three options. While heuristic approaches can be useful in certain situations, they can also lead to biased or incomplete solutions if they are not used carefully.

Creativity is also an important factor in effective problem solving, as it allows individuals to generate novel and innovative ideas and approaches to complex problems. Creativity involves the ability to think outside the box, to see connections and patterns that others may not see, and to come up with original solutions to problems. Creativity can be developed and nurtured through activities such as brainstorming, asking open-ended questions, and encouraging exploration and experimentation.

Collaboration is another important factor in effective problem solving, as it allows individuals to share ideas and perspectives, and to draw on the expertise and experience of others. Collaboration can involve working with others in person or online, and can involve a variety of different approaches such as group brainstorming, project management software, and online collaboration tools. Collaboration can be particularly useful when faced with complex, multi-faceted problems, as it allows individuals to draw on a wide range of knowledge and experience to find the best possible solution.

In conclusion, there are a variety of approaches to problem solving, each with its own set of theories and practical applications. Linear approaches are well suited to problems with clear, objective solutions, while non-linear approaches are better suited to complex, dynamic problems. Heuristic approaches provide a framework for decision making in unfamiliar situations, while creativity and collaboration allow individuals to generate novel ideas and draw on the expertise and experience of others. Regardless of the approach used, effective problem solving requires a combination of analytical and creative thinking, as well as the ability to identify and address the root causes of problems.

Chapter

7

DEVELOPING YOUR COMMUNICATION SKILLS

Developing your communication skills as an adjuster is crucial in order to effectively communicate with policyholders, claimants, and colleagues. There are several approaches you can take to improve your communication skills, including learning about different communication theories and applying practical strategies.

One approach is to understand the basic principles of effective communication. According to the Social Exchange Theory, communication is a process of giving and receiving information with the goal of achieving mutual satisfaction. This means that effective communication involves listening and understanding the perspective of the other person, as well as expressing your own thoughts and feelings clearly and concisely.

Another important aspect of effective communication is nonverbal cues. According to the Nonverbal Communication Theory, nonverbal cues such as facial expressions, body language, and tone of voice can convey important information and influence how a message is perceived. As an adjuster, it is important to be aware of your own nonverbal cues and how they may be interpreted by others. You should also pay attention to the nonverbal cues of the person you are communicating with in order to better understand their thoughts and feelings.

One of the best strategies for improving your communication skills is to actively listen, which we've mentioned a few times already in this book, but it's worth repeating. Active listening involves paying attention to what the other person is saying, asking clarifying questions, and providing feedback. This can help to ensure that you fully understand the other person's perspective and can respond appropriately. You should also strive to be empathetic, which means trying to see things from the other person's perspective and showing understanding and compassion.

Another approach to improving your communication skills is to learn about different communication styles. According to the Communication Styles Theory, there are four main communication styles: passive, aggressive, passive-aggressive, and assertive. Passive communication involves avoiding expressing your own thoughts and feelings, while aggressive communication involves expressing your thoughts and feelings in a way that is dominating or confrontational. Passive-aggressive communication involves expressing your thoughts and feelings indirectly, while assertive communication involves expressing your thoughts and feelings in a confident and respectful manner. As an adjuster, it is important to aim for assertive communication, as it allows you to express your thoughts and feelings while still respecting the rights and needs of others.

One practical strategy for improving your communication skills is to use "I" statements. "I" statements involve expressing your thoughts and feelings in a way that focuses on your own perspective, rather than blaming or accusing the other person. For example, instead of saying "You always make me feel incompetent," you might say "I feel frustrated and upset when I am not able to complete tasks to the best of my ability." Using "I" statements can help to prevent misunderstandings and conflicts and can make it easier for the other person to understand and respond to your thoughts and feelings.

Another approach to improving your communication skills is to learn about different conflict resolution strategies. According to the Conflict Resolution Theory, there are five main approaches to resolving conflicts: avoidance, accommodation, compromise, competition, and collaboration. Avoidance involves avoiding the conflict altogether, while accommodation involves giving in to the other person's demands. Compromise involves both parties giving up something in order to reach a resolution, while competition involves trying to win the conflict at all costs. Collaboration involves working together to find a solution that meets the needs of both parties. As an adjuster, it is important to aim for collaboration, as it allows you to find a resolution that is mutually beneficial and can help to strengthen your relationships with others.

One practical strategy for improving your communication skills is to use reflective listening. Reflective listening involves restating what the other person has said in your own words, in order to show that you have understood their perspective. This can help to reduce misunderstandings and can make it easier for the other person to feel heard and understood.

In this chapter, we discussed the importance of developing effective communication skills as an adjuster. We explored different communication theories, such as active listening, assertiveness, and empathy, and how they can help you communicate more effectively with policyholders, claimants, and colleagues. We also looked at practical strategies for improving your communication skills, such as paying attention to body language, using clear and concise language, and seeking feedback from others. By taking the time to develop and hone your communication skills, you can improve your ability to effectively communicate with others and be a more successful adjuster.

Chapter 8

EMOTIONAL INTELLIGENCE

Emotional intelligence (EI) refers to the ability to recognize and understand one's own emotions and the emotions of others, and to use this awareness to manage and regulate emotions in oneself and in relationships. It is a critical skill for adjusters, as it allows them to effectively communicate and build trust with clients, colleagues, and other stakeholders. In this chapter, we will explore the theories and practical applications of EI in the context of adjusters, and provide tips on how to cultivate and enhance this skill.

Theories of Emotional Intelligence

One of the earliest theories of EI was proposed by Peter Salovey and John Mayer in 1990, who defined it as a set of cognitive and emotional skills that involve the ability to perceive, express, understand, and regulate emotions. According to this model, EI consists of five main components: emotional perception, emotional expression, emotional understanding, emotional regulation, and emotional relationships.

Another influential theory of EI was developed by Daniel Goleman in 1995, who defined it as the ability to recognize and understand emotions in oneself and others, and to use this awareness to manage and regulate emotions in oneself and in relationships. Goleman's model includes four main competencies: self-awareness, self-regulation, motivation, and social skills. Self-awareness refers to the ability to recognize one's own emotions and how they affect thoughts and behaviors. It involves being attuned to one's own emotional states and how they may impact others.

Self-regulation refers to the ability to manage and control one's own emotions, thoughts, and behaviors in order to achieve a desired outcome. It involves being able to manage impulses, set goals, and take appropriate actions in response to emotions. Motivation refers to the ability to use emotions to drive and sustain action towards a desired goal. It involves being able to harness positive emotions, such as enthusiasm and excitement, to achieve success.

Social skills refer to the ability to effectively communicate and build relationships with others. It involves being able to understand and respond appropriately to the emotions of others, and to use this understanding to build trust and establish positive relationships.

Practical Applications of Emotional Intelligence for Adjusters

Emotional intelligence is a valuable skill for adjusters, as it allows them to effectively communicate and build trust with clients, colleagues, and other stakeholders. Some specific ways in which EI can be applied in the context of adjusters include:

1. Communication and conflict resolution: Adjusters often

have to deal with clients who are upset or distressed due to the circumstances that led to their claim. EI can help adjusters to effectively communicate with these clients, and to understand and respond appropriately to their emotions. It can also help adjusters to de-escalate conflicts and find mutually beneficial solutions.

2. Building trust and rapport: Adjusters work with clients who may be skeptical or mistrusting, especially if they are dealing with a complex or contentious claim. EI can help adjusters to build trust and rapport by showing empathy and understanding, and by being transparent and honest in their interactions.

3. Teamwork and collaboration: Adjusters often work as part of a team, and EI can help them to effectively collaborate with their colleagues and other stakeholders. It can help adjusters to understand and respond appropriately to the emotions of their teammates, and to use this understanding to build a positive and productive work environment.

4. Adaptability and resilience: Adjusters may face unexpected challenges or setbacks in their work, and EI can help them to adapt and bounce back from these challenges. It can help adjusters to manage their own emotions and to remain calm and focused.

Professionalism and verbal and nonverbal communication

As an insurance adjuster, professionalism is crucial in order to effectively handle the various tasks and responsibilities that come with the job. This includes not only technical skills and knowledge, but also the ability to manage and understand one's own emotions, as well as those of others. This is where emotional intelligence comes into play.

Emotional intelligence is the ability to recognize, understand, and manage one's own emotions, as well as the emotions of others. It involves being aware of one's own feelings and how they influence behavior, as well as being able to effectively communicate and empathize with others.

For adjusters, emotional intelligence is especially important when interacting with clients who may be experiencing a stressful or difficult situation. It is essential to be able to understand and respond to their emotions in a compassionate and professional manner, rather than becoming overwhelmed or reacting negatively.

In addition to interacting with clients, emotional intelligence is also important in managing relationships with colleagues and supervisors. Being able to effectively communicate and understand the emotions of others can help to create a positive and productive work environment.

Emotional intelligence can also be beneficial in the decision-making process. Being able to recognize and understand one's own emotions can help to prevent impulsive or rash decisions, and instead allow for more logical and thought-out choices.

Developing emotional intelligence can take time and effort, but it is a valuable skill that can greatly enhance professionalism as an adjuster. Some ways to improve emotional intelligence include:

- Practicing self-awareness and self-regulation: This involves being aware of and managing one's own emotions, as well as being able to control impulsive reactions.

- Improving empathy: This involves being able to understand and respond to the emotions of others, and being able to put oneself in someone else's shoes.

- Enhancing social skills: This includes being able to effectively communicate and build relationships with others, as well as being able to effectively manage conflict.

- Seeking feedback and learning from others: Asking for feedback from colleagues and supervisors can help to identify areas where emotional intelligence may need improvement, and learning from others who exhibit strong emotional intelligence can be beneficial.

Overall, emotional intelligence is a crucial aspect of professionalism for adjusters. It allows for better communication, understanding, and relationship management with clients, colleagues, and supervisors, ultimately leading to more effective and successful work. By continuously developing and improving emotional intelligence, adjusters can become more effective and professional in their roles.

Chapter 9

EMPATHY

Empathy is a critical skill for adjusters, as it allows them to understand and relate to the experiences and emotions of others. This understanding can help adjusters to more effectively assess and address the needs of policyholders and claimants, leading to better outcomes and higher levels of satisfaction.

There are several theories that have been proposed to explain empathy and how it works. One of the most well-known is the cognitive empathy theory, which suggests that empathy involves the ability to take on the perspective of others and understand their thoughts and feelings. Another theory is the emotional empathy theory, which suggests that empathy involves the ability to feel what others are feeling.

Regardless of which theory is most accurate, it is clear that empathy plays a crucial role in the ability of adjusters to effectively communicate with and support policyholders and claimants. This is especially important in times of crisis, when individuals may be experiencing high levels of stress and emotional distress.

There are several practical applications of empathy in the field of insurance adjusting. For example, adjusters can use empathy to better understand the needs and concerns of policyholders and claimants, and to develop strategies to address these needs. Adjusters can also use empathy to identify and address any underlying issues or concerns that may be contributing to a policyholder's or claimant's distress.

One important aspect of using empathy as an adjuster is the ability to listen actively and attentively to what the policyholder or claimant is saying. This means not just hearing the words that are being spoken, but also paying attention to nonverbal cues such as body language and facial expressions. Active listening allows adjusters to better understand the perspective of the policyholder or claimant, and to identify any areas of concern or uncertainty.

Adjusters can also use empathy to build trust and rapport with policyholders and claimants. By demonstrating a genuine understanding of their experiences and emotions, adjusters can help to establish a sense of trust and credibility, which is essential for building strong relationships with clients.

There are several case studies that illustrate the importance of empathy in the field of insurance adjusting. One such case involves a policyholder who had recently experienced a fire in their home. The policyholder was understandably upset and anxious about the situation, and was struggling to navigate the claims process.

In this case, the adjuster was able to use empathy to understand the policyholder's perspective and to provide the necessary support and guidance. By listening actively and attentively to the policyholder's concerns, the adjuster was able to identify and address any underlying issues or concerns. The adjuster was also able to provide emotional support to the policyholder, helping to alleviate their anxiety and stress.

Overall, the use of empathy was key to the success of this case, as it allowed the adjuster to effectively assess and address the needs of the policyholder, leading to a more positive outcome.

Another case study involves a policyholder who had experienced significant damage to their property due to a natural disaster. In this case, the adjuster was able to use empathy to better understand the policyholder's experience and to provide the necessary support and guidance.

By actively listening to the policyholder's concerns and taking the time to understand their perspective, the adjuster was able to identify and address any underlying issues or concerns. The adjuster was also able to provide emotional support to the policyholder, helping to alleviate their stress and anxiety.

Overall, the use of empathy was critical to the success of this case, as it allowed the adjuster to effectively assess and address the needs of the policyholder, leading to a more positive outcome. Empathy is a crucial skill for insurance adjusters, as it allows them to understand and relate to the experiences and emotions of others.

Chapter 10

TIME MANAGEMENT

Time management is a critical skill for adjusters to master, as they are often faced with tight deadlines, competing priorities, and a high volume of claims to process. Adjusters who can effectively manage their time are able to work more efficiently, meet deadlines, and provide better service to clients.

There are several theories and approaches to time management that can be helpful for adjusters to consider. One popular theory is the Pareto principle, also known as the 80/20 rule. This principle states that roughly 80% of the effects come from 20% of the causes. In terms of time management, this means that 20% of an adjuster's tasks will likely take up 80% of their time. By identifying and focusing on these high-impact tasks, adjusters can prioritize their workload and make the most of their time.

Another time management theory is the Eisenhower matrix, which helps adjusters prioritize tasks based on their importance and urgency. This matrix divides tasks into four quadrants:

important and urgent, important but not urgent, urgent but not important, and neither urgent nor important. Adjusters should focus on tasks in the first quadrant first, followed by tasks in the second quadrant, and so on. This helps adjusters prioritize their workload and avoid wasting time on tasks that are not important or urgent.

Practical applications of time management for adjusters include setting goals and creating a plan of action. Setting clear goals can help adjusters stay focused and motivated, and a plan of action can help them break down tasks into smaller, more manageable steps. Adjusters should also consider using tools like calendars, to-do lists, and project management software to help them stay organized and on track.

Another practical tip for adjusters is to batch similar tasks together. For example, instead of constantly switching between tasks, adjusters can group similar tasks together and work on them in one sitting. This can help them stay focused and avoid wasting time switching between tasks.

Adjusters should also be mindful of how they allocate their time and energy. For example, they should be strategic about when they tackle high-energy tasks, such as complex claims or difficult clients. These tasks should be done during the times of day when the adjuster has the most energy and focus. Adjusters should also be aware of their energy levels throughout the day and take breaks as needed to recharge.

One common time-waster for adjusters is unnecessary meetings and emails. To avoid these time-sinks, adjusters should be selective about the meetings they attend and try to keep emails short and to the point. They should also consider setting boundaries around their work time and communication, such as not checking emails after a certain time in the evening.

Another way adjusters can improve their time management is by delegating tasks to others. Adjusters should be aware of their strengths and limitations, and be willing to delegate tasks that they are not well-suited for or that could be done more efficiently by someone else. This can free up time for the adjuster to focus on more important tasks and improve overall productivity.

In summary, time management is an essential skill for adjusters to master in order to work efficiently, meet deadlines, and provide excellent service to clients. Adjusters can benefit from theories such as the Pareto principle and the Eisenhower matrix, as well as practical tips such as setting goals, creating a plan of action, batching tasks, and delegating tasks. By being mindful of how they allocate their time and energy, adjusters can improve their productivity and achieve their goals.

Professionalism and Time management

Time management is a critical aspect of professionalism for adjusters. Adjusters often have to juggle multiple tasks and priorities, and it is important to be able to manage one's time effectively in order to get everything done in a timely and efficient manner.

There are a few key strategies that adjusters can use to improve their time management skills:

1. Set clear goals and priorities. Before starting any task, it is important to have a clear understanding of what needs to be done and why it is important. This can help adjusters prioritize their tasks and allocate their time accordingly.

2. Create a schedule and stick to it. Having a schedule can help adjusters stay organized and ensure that they are

making the most of their time. It is important to be realistic when creating a schedule and to allow for some flexibility in case unexpected events or emergencies arise.

3. Manage distractions. Distractions can be a major hindrance to productivity, so it is important to minimize them as much as possible. This might mean setting aside dedicated times for checking email or social media, or finding a quiet place to work where you can focus without interruptions.

4. Use tools and technologies to your advantage. There are many tools and technologies available that can help adjusters manage their time more effectively. For example, project management software can help adjusters keep track of tasks and deadlines, and time tracking software can help adjusters see where they are spending the most time and identify areas where they can be more efficient.

5. Take breaks and practice self-care. It is important to remember to take breaks and practice self-care in order to stay focused and productive. This might involve taking short breaks to stretch or get some fresh air, or making time for activities like exercise or meditation.

By implementing these strategies, adjusters can improve their time management skills and be more professional in their work.

Chapter

11

TEAMWORK

Teamwork is a crucial element in the success of any organization, and this is especially true for adjusters who are often working on complex and time-sensitive claims. The ability to collaborate effectively with colleagues and clients can mean the difference between a smoothly processed claim and one that becomes bogged down in delays and misunderstandings.

There are several theories and models that can help adjusters understand how to work effectively as a team. One of the most well-known is Tuckman's stages of group development, which proposes that teams go through five stages of development: forming, storming, norming, performing, and adjourning.

In the forming stage, team members are getting to know each other and establishing roles and expectations. During this stage, it is important for the team leader to set clear goals and establish communication channels. It is also important for team members to be open and honest about their strengths and weaknesses, and to establish trust and respect among team members.

The storming stage is often the most challenging, as team members may start to challenge each other and the team leader, and conflicts may arise. It is important for the team leader to remain calm and to encourage open communication, as well as to establish clear guidelines for resolving conflicts.

The norming stage is when the team starts to work together more effectively and begins to establish routines and processes. This is a critical stage for building trust and cohesion, and team members should be encouraged to support and help each other.

The performing stage is when the team is working at its highest level of productivity and effectiveness. At this stage, team members should be able to collaborate effectively, communicate openly and honestly, and work towards a common goal.

The adjourning stage is when the team is disbanded or the project is completed. It is important for team members to reflect on the successes and challenges of the project, and to share any lessons learned.

Another important theory for understanding teamwork is Belbin's Team Role Theory, which proposes that individuals have distinct roles that they are best suited for within a team. These roles include:

- The coordinator: This person is responsible for organizing the team and ensuring that everyone is working towards the same goal. They are often good at delegating tasks and keeping the team on track.

- The shaper: This person is driven and energetic, and is often the one who pushes the team to achieve its goals. They are good at problem-solving and coming up with creative solutions.

- The implementer: This person is practical and organized, and is good at turning ideas into action. They are responsible for making sure that tasks are completed efficiently and on time.

- The finisher: This person is detail-oriented and focused on getting things done. They are responsible for ensuring that all tasks are completed to a high standard.

- The specialist: This person is an expert in a particular area and is responsible for bringing their expertise to the team. They may be relied upon to provide technical or specialized knowledge.

- The monitor-evaluator: This person is analytical and objective, and is responsible for assessing the team's progress and suggesting improvements.

- The team worker: This person is good at building relationships and facilitating communication within the team. They are responsible for keeping the team cohesive and working towards a common goal.

By understanding these different roles, adjusters can better understand how to work effectively with their colleagues and contribute to the team in meaningful ways.

One practical application of teamwork in the field of adjusting is the use of team huddles. These daily or weekly meetings provide an opportunity for team members to come together, share updates and challenges, and collaborate on solutions.

Teamwork is an essential component of any successful business, and this is especially true for adjusters. Adjusters are responsible for working with insurance clients to assess and manage the claims process in the event of a loss or damage. This often involves working with a team of other adjusters, underwriters, claims managers, and other professionals to ensure that the claims process is handled efficiently and effectively.

There are many practical applications of teamwork for adjusters, and some of the most important are outlined below.

1. Improved communication and collaboration

Effective teamwork requires good communication and collaboration between team members. This is especially important for adjusters, as they often work with clients who are going through a difficult time due to a loss or damage. By working as a team, adjusters can ensure that all parties are kept informed about the claims process and that any issues or concerns are addressed promptly.

2. Enhanced problem-solving abilities

Adjusters often face complex and challenging situations that require creative problem-solving skills. By working as a team, adjusters can pool their knowledge, expertise, and resources to identify the best solutions to complex problems. This can help to minimize delays and improve the overall efficiency of the claims process.

3. Increased efficiency and productivity

Teamwork can help to streamline the claims process by allowing adjusters to divide tasks and responsibilities among team members. This can help to reduce workloads and increase efficiency, as team members can focus on their areas of expertise and expertise. By working together, adjusters can also identify and address bottlenecks or other inefficiencies in the process, further improving productivity.

4. Enhanced customer service

Adjusters who work as part of a team can provide a more comprehensive and efficient service to clients. This can help to improve customer satisfaction and loyalty, as clients feel that their needs are being met in a timely and effective manner.

5. Improved team morale and retention

Teamwork can also have a positive impact on team morale and retention. When team members feel that they are valued and supported, they are more likely to be motivated and engaged in their work. This can lead to higher levels of job satisfaction and a reduced risk of turnover.

6. Greater flexibility and adaptability

Teamwork can also help to increase the flexibility and adaptability of an adjuster team. By working together, team members can share knowledge and resources, allowing them to respond more quickly to changing circumstances or client needs. This can help to ensure that the claims process remains efficient and effective, even in times of high demand or unexpected challenges.

7. Enhanced professional development

Working as part of a team can also provide opportunities for professional development. Team members can learn from each other, share best practices, and provide support and mentorship to one another. This can help to build skills and knowledge, and can lead to career advancement for team members.

8. Improved team dynamics

Effective teamwork requires a positive and supportive team dynamic. When team members feel that they are valued and respected, and that their contributions are valued, they are more likely to be motivated and engaged in their work. This can help to foster a sense of teamwork and collaboration, which can lead to better outcomes for clients and the organization.

9. Greater accountability and responsibility

Teamwork can also increase accountability and responsibility among team members. When team members work together to achieve common goals, they are more likely to be held accountable for their actions and contributions. This can help to promote a culture of responsibility and accountability, which can lead to better outcomes for clients and the organization.

10. Enhanced resilience and flexibility

Finally, teamwork can help to enhance the resilience and flexibility of an adjuster.

In this chapter, we explored the importance of teamwork in the claims adjusting process and highlighted some key strategies for building and maintaining effective teams. These strategies included:

- Communication: The ability to communicate clearly and effectively is crucial for building trust and cooperation within a team.

- Collaboration: Working together to solve problems and make decisions is essential for moving claims forward efficiently.

- Empathy: Understanding and being sensitive to the needs and concerns of others can help build trust and create a positive work environment.

- Flexibility: The ability to adapt to changing circumstances and work with others to find creative solutions can be a key factor in the success of any team.

Overall, teamwork is a critical component of the claims adjusting process, and by implementing these strategies, adjusters can work together to achieve the best possible outcomes for clients and the organization.

Chapter 12

GOALS, DEADLINES, AND WORKLOAD

As an adjuster, it is essential to prioritize your workload and set clear goals and deadlines in order to stay organized and efficient. With numerous claims to manage and a variety of tasks to complete, it can be overwhelming to keep track of everything. However, by using various techniques and tools, you can effectively prioritize your workload, set goals, and meet deadlines while maintaining a sense of organization.

One effective technique for prioritizing your workload is to use the urgent-important matrix. This matrix consists of four quadrants: urgent and important, important but not urgent, urgent but not important, and not urgent and not important. By evaluating each task according to its level of importance and urgency, you can prioritize your workload and focus on the tasks that are most important and pressing.

For example, tasks that are both urgent and important, such as attending a meeting with a client or completing a report by a specific deadline, should be given the highest priority. Tasks that are important but not urgent, such as reviewing policies or updating your skills, should also be given a high priority, as they may become urgent if not completed in a timely manner. Tasks that are urgent but not important, such as responding to emails from colleagues, should be given a lower priority, as they can be delegated or completed at a later time. Tasks that are not urgent and not important, such as browsing social media or checking emails for leisure, should be avoided altogether or completed only after all other tasks have been completed.

Another technique for prioritizing your workload is to use the ABCDE method. This method involves assigning each task a letter based on its level of importance. Tasks that are considered A tasks are the most important and should be completed first. These tasks may include meeting with clients, reviewing policies, or completing reports. B tasks are important but not as pressing as A tasks and should be completed after A tasks are finished. C tasks are less important and should be completed after A and B tasks. D tasks are tasks that can be delegated or postponed, and E tasks are tasks that can be eliminated altogether.

In addition to prioritizing your workload, it is essential to set clear goals and deadlines for each task. This can help you stay focused and motivated, as well as ensure that tasks are completed in a timely manner. To set goals and deadlines, it is helpful to use the SMART criteria. SMART stands for Specific, Measurable, Achievable, Relevant, and Time-bound. By setting goals that are specific, measurable, achievable, relevant, and time-bound, you can ensure that your goals are clear and attainable.

For example, instead of setting a goal to "complete all claims," a specific and measurable goal might be "complete all claims within three business days of receipt." This goal is specific, as it clearly defines the task to be completed, and it is measurable, as it provides a clear timeframe for completion. It is also achievable, as it is within a realistic timeframe, and relevant, as it aligns with the needs of the business. By setting clear goals and deadlines, you can stay focused and motivated, as well as ensure that tasks are completed efficiently.

To stay organized and manage your workload effectively, it is also essential to use tools such as calendars and to-do lists. Calendars can help you keep track of deadlines, appointments, and other important dates, while to-do lists can help you prioritize and organize your tasks.

One helpful tool for managing your workload is a digital calendar, such as Google Calendar or Outlook Calendar. These calendars allow you to easily schedule appointments, set reminders, and view your schedule in a variety of formats, such as a daily, weekly, or monthly view. Calendars and to-do lists are two essential tools for staying organized, especially for adjusters who often have a lot on their plate. By using these tools effectively, adjusters can better manage their time, prioritize tasks, and stay on top of their workload.

One technique for using calendars to stay organized is to create a master calendar that includes all of your appointments, meetings, and deadlines. This calendar should be accessible from any device, such as a phone, tablet, or computer, so that you can easily reference it wherever you are. You can also use the calendar to schedule blocks of time for specific tasks or projects, such as reviewing a claim or preparing a report.

Another technique is to use the calendar to set reminders for yourself. For example, you can set a reminder to follow up on a claim a week after it was submitted, or to review a report the day before a meeting. Reminders can help you stay on track and ensure that you don't forget important tasks or deadlines.

To-do lists are another useful tool for staying organized. You can use a to-do list to keep track of all of the tasks you need to complete in a given day, week, or month. To-do lists can be created digitally, using a task management app or software, or you can use a paper-based system, such as a notebook or planner.

One technique for using to-do lists effectively is to prioritize your tasks. You can do this by assigning a priority level to each task, such as "high," "medium," or "low." This can help you focus on the most important tasks first and avoid getting bogged down in less important ones. You can also use to-do lists to break larger tasks down into smaller, more manageable steps. This can make it easier to track your progress and stay motivated.

Another technique is to review your to-do list regularly and adjust it as needed. This can help you stay up to date on your tasks and ensure that you are making progress towards your goals. You can also use your to-do list to keep track of tasks that are complete and check them off as you go. This can help you stay motivated and give you a sense of accomplishment as you work through your list.

In addition to calendars and to-do lists, there are several other tools and techniques that can help adjusters stay organized. These include:

- Time management techniques: There are many different time management techniques that can help adjusters stay organized and manage their time effectively. Some examples include the Pomodoro Technique, which involves working in short bursts with breaks in between, and the

Eisenhower Matrix, which helps you prioritize tasks based on their importance and urgency.

- Note-taking tools: Adjusters often need to take notes during meetings or while reviewing claims, so it's important to have a reliable system for capturing and organizing this information. Tools like Evernote or OneNote can be useful for this purpose, as they allow you to create digital notebooks and tag or categorize your notes for easy reference later.

- Project management software: For larger projects or cases, project management software can be a helpful tool for keeping track of tasks, deadlines, and progress. Tools like Asana or Trello allow you to create project boards and assign tasks to team members, as well as track progress and communicate with others involved in the project.

Overall, using tools like calendars and to-do lists, as well as other time management and organization techniques, can help adjusters stay on top of their workload and be more efficient and effective in their work. By taking the time to plan and organize their tasks, adjusters can better manage their time and prioritize their workload.

Professionalism and prioritizing your workload and setting clear goals and deadlines

As an adjuster, it is important to prioritize your workload and set clear goals and deadlines to ensure that you are able to handle all of the tasks assigned to you efficiently and effectively. This level of professionalism is essential in order to meet the expectations of clients, colleagues, and superiors.

One way to prioritize your workload is to use a task management system, such as Trello or Asana. These tools allow you to create a list of tasks and assign them a priority level, such as high, medium, or low. This allows you to focus on the most important tasks first and ensure that you are able to complete them before moving on to less pressing matters.

In addition to prioritizing your workload, it is also important to set clear goals and deadlines for each task. This helps to ensure that you are able to complete each task in a timely manner and meet the expectations of your clients and colleagues. When setting goals and deadlines, be sure to consider the resources that you have available and the amount of time that you have to complete the task. This will help you to set realistic goals and deadlines that are achievable within the given timeframe.

To further enhance your level of professionalism as an adjuster, it is important to communicate your goals and deadlines with your clients and colleagues. This helps to ensure that everyone is on the same page and working towards the same objectives. You may also want to consider setting up regular check-ins or progress reports to ensure that you are meeting your goals and deadlines.

In conclusion, prioritizing your workload and setting clear goals and deadlines are essential for professionalism as an adjuster. By using task management tools and communicating your objectives with clients and colleagues, you can ensure that you are able to handle all of your tasks efficiently and effectively. This level of professionalism will help to build trust and credibility with your clients and colleagues and ensure that you are able to meet their expectations.

Chapter 13

NAVIGATING LEGAL AND REGULATORY ISSUES

As an insurance adjuster, it is important to be aware of the various legal and regulatory issues that you may encounter in your line of work. These issues can arise when handling claims, communicating with clients, and working with insurance companies. In this chapter, we will provide some tips for navigating these issues and staying compliant with relevant laws and regulations.

1. Familiarize yourself with relevant laws and regulations one of the first steps you can take to navigate legal and regulatory issues as an insurance adjuster is to familiarize yourself with the laws and regulations that apply to your work. This may include state insurance laws, federal insurance regulations, and industry-specific guidelines.

2. Understand your role and responsibilities as an insurance adjuster, you have certain responsibilities to your clients, insurance company, and the policyholder. It is important to understand what is expected of you in each of these

roles and to act in a way that is consistent with your responsibilities.

3. Maintain confidentiality when handling claims, you may have access to sensitive personal and financial information. It is important to maintain confidentiality and protect this information from unauthorized disclosure. You should also be aware of any privacy laws or regulations that may apply to your work, such as the Health Insurance Portability and Accountability Act (HIPAA) or the General Data Protection Regulation (GDPR).

4. Communicate clearly and accurately effective communication is key to navigating legal and regulatory issues as an insurance adjuster. When communicating with clients, policyholders, and other stakeholders, it is important to be clear and accurate in your messaging. This includes accurately conveying information about the claim, policy terms, and any limitations or exclusions that may apply.

5. Stay up to date on industry developments the insurance industry is constantly evolving, and it is important for adjusters to stay up to date on new developments and changes to laws and regulations. This can help you navigate legal and regulatory issues and ensure that you are providing the best possible service to your clients.

6. Seek legal guidance when needed if you are unsure about how to handle a particular legal or regulatory issue, it may be helpful to seek guidance from a legal professional. This could include an attorney who specializes in insurance law or a compliance officer within your company.

7. Maintain proper documentation proper documentation is important for navigating legal and regulatory issues as an insurance adjuster. This includes keeping accurate and complete records of all claims-related activities, such as communication with clients and policyholders, evaluations of damages, and any payments made. Proper documentation can help protect you and your company in the event of a legal dispute or regulatory investigation.

8. Be aware of potential conflicts of interest as an insurance adjuster, it is important to be aware of potential conflicts of interest that may arise in your work. This could include situations where you have a personal or financial interest in the outcome of a claim, or where you may have a relationship with a policyholder or client that could influence your judgment. If you are aware of a potential conflict of interest, you should disclose it to your supervisor or compliance officer and follow any guidelines for managing the conflict.

In conclusion, navigating legal and regulatory issues as an insurance adjuster requires a thorough understanding of relevant laws and regulations, as well as effective communication and careful documentation. By following these tips and seeking guidance when needed, you can ensure that you are complying with legal and regulatory requirements and providing the best possible service to your clients.

Chapter

14

QUESTIONING TECHNIQUES

Questioning techniques are a critical element of the claims adjusting process. Adjusters must be able to effectively and efficiently gather information from claimants, witnesses, and other parties in order to accurately assess the validity of a claim and determine the appropriate course of action. In this context, questioning techniques can be thought of as a set of tools that adjusters can use to facilitate the gathering of information and to ensure that they have a clear understanding of the details and circumstances surrounding a claim.

There are several different theories and approaches to questioning techniques that can be applied in the context of claims adjusting. Some of the key theories and approaches include the following:

1. The cognitive interviewing approach: This approach to questioning techniques is based on the idea that people have a limited capacity for remembering and recalling

events and information. The cognitive interviewing approach aims to optimize the memory and recall of information by using specific questioning techniques and strategies. This approach typically involves using open-ended questions, asking questions in a specific order, and using prompts and prompts to facilitate recall.

2. The structured interviewing approach: This approach to questioning techniques involves using a set of predetermined questions to gather information from claimants and other parties. The structured interviewing approach is particularly useful when gathering standardized information, such as demographic data or information about a specific event or incident.

3. The motivational interviewing approach: This approach to questioning techniques is based on the idea that people are more likely to engage in behaviors that are consistent with their values and goals. Motivational interviewing involves using open-ended questions and reflective listening to help claimants identify their own motivations and goals, and to explore the potential benefits and drawbacks of different options and courses of action.

4. The confrontation approach: This approach to questioning techniques involves using direct and confrontational questioning to challenge the accuracy or validity of information provided by claimants and other parties. The confrontation approach is typically used when there are discrepancies or inconsistencies in the information provided, or when there is reason to believe that the information provided may not be entirely accurate.

In order to effectively apply these and other questioning

techniques in the context of claims adjusting, it is important for adjusters to have a thorough understanding of the theories and principles underlying these approaches. It is also important for adjusters to be able to adapt and modify their questioning techniques as needed based on the specific circumstances and needs of each claim.

One key factor that can impact the effectiveness of questioning techniques in claims adjusting is the rapport and trust between the adjuster and the claimant or other parties being questioned. It is important for adjusters to establish a sense of trust and rapport with claimants and other parties in order to facilitate open and honest communication. This can be achieved through active listening, using non-threatening and non-judgmental language, and demonstrating genuine concern and empathy.

Another key factor that can impact the effectiveness of questioning techniques in claims adjusting is the ability to ask the right questions at the right time. Adjusters should be able to identify the most important and relevant questions to ask based on the specific circumstances of each claim. This may involve asking open-ended questions to gather additional information, asking follow-up questions to clarify or expand upon previous answers, or using prompts and prompts to facilitate recall.

In addition to these general principles, there are also several specific questioning techniques that adjusters can use to effectively gather information and assess the validity of a claim. Some of the key questioning techniques that adjusters can use include the following:

1. Open-ended questions: These are questions that cannot be answered with a simple "yes" or "no" response. Open-ended questions encourage claimants to provide more

detailed and thorough responses, which can be helpful in gathering a full understanding of the situation. Examples of open-ended questions include: "Can you tell me more about what happened?", "How did the accident occur?", and "What damages or injuries did you sustain as a result of the accident?"

2. Closed-ended questions: These are questions that can be answered with a simple "yes" or "no" response, or with a specific piece of information. Closed-ended questions can be useful for gathering specific details or clarifying information, but should be used in conjunction with open-ended questions to get a full understanding of the situation. Examples of closed-ended questions include: "Were you wearing a seatbelt at the time of the accident?", "Did you seek medical attention after the accident?", and "Is your vehicle currently drivable?"

3. Probing questions: These are questions that follow up on a previous answer, or that delve deeper into a particular topic. Probing questions can help adjusters gather additional information and clarify any confusion or uncertainty. Examples of probing questions include: "Can you explain what you meant by that?", "Can you give me more details about the damages to your vehicle?", and "What specific injuries did you sustain in the accident?"

4. Leading questions: These are questions that suggest a particular answer or bias. Leading questions should be avoided, as they can influence a claimant's response and potentially undermine the accuracy and fairness of the claims process. Examples of leading questions include: "You weren't at fault for the accident, were you?", "You didn't suffer any serious injuries, did you?", and "You don't have any prior accidents on your record, do you?"

5. Clarifying questions: These are questions that seek to clarify or confirm information that has already been provided. Clarifying questions can be helpful in ensuring that the adjuster fully understands the claimant's responses and can make informed decisions about the claim. Examples of clarifying questions include: "Could you clarify what you meant by that?", "Could you confirm the date of the accident?", and "Could you provide the make and model of your vehicle?"

6. Follow-up questions: These are questions that are asked after the initial questioning has been completed, in order to gather additional information or clarify any remaining issues. Follow-up questions can be helpful in ensuring that all necessary information has been gathered and all issues have been addressed. Examples of follow-up questions include: "Is there anything else you think I should know?", "Do you have any questions for me?", and "Is there anyone else who may have information relevant to the claim?"

In conclusion, adjusters can use a variety of questioning techniques to effectively gather accurate and relevant information during the claims process. These techniques include open-ended questions, closed-ended questions, probing questions, clarifying questions, and follow-up questions. It is important for adjusters to use these techniques in a fair and unbiased manner, and to avoid using leading questions that may influence a claimant's response. By using these techniques effectively, adjusters can ensure that they have all necessary information to make informed decisions about the claim.

Chapter 15

DEALING WITH DIFFICULT CLIENTS AND SITUATIONS

As an insurance adjuster, dealing with difficult clients and situations is an inevitable part of the job. Whether it's a disgruntled policyholder who is upset about their claim being denied, or a natural disaster that has caused widespread damage and stress for those affected, it's important for adjusters to be able to handle these situations with professionalism and empathy.

One of the most common difficulties that adjusters face is dealing with policyholders who are upset about their claim being denied. This can often be a frustrating and emotional experience for the policyholder, and it's important for adjusters to approach these situations with understanding and patience.

One way to handle these situations is to be transparent and honest with the policyholder. Explain the reasoning behind the claim denial and provide clear explanations of the policy terms and conditions. It's also important to listen to the policyholder's concerns and address any issues they may have.

Another strategy is to offer solutions and alternatives. If the claim is denied due to a policy exclusion, it may be helpful to discuss other coverage options that the policyholder may have. It may also be useful to refer the policyholder to other resources or organizations that may be able to assist them.

It's also important for adjusters to be aware of their own emotions when dealing with difficult clients. It can be easy to become frustrated or annoyed when a policyholder is upset or angry, but it's important to remain professional and calm in order to effectively resolve the issue.

In situations where a policyholder becomes aggressive or confrontational, it may be necessary to set boundaries and establish clear expectations for communication. This can involve stating that the conversation will not continue until the policyholder is able to speak calmly and respectfully.

Another difficult situation that adjusters may face is dealing with natural disasters, such as hurricanes, earthquakes, and wildfires. These events can cause widespread damage and chaos, and policyholders may be overwhelmed and stressed as they deal with the aftermath.

In these situations, it's important for adjusters to be compassionate and understanding. Many policyholders may be dealing with loss and trauma, and it's important to recognize and acknowledge these emotions.

One way to handle these situations is to provide support and assistance to policyholders as they navigate the claims process.

This can involve providing clear explanations of the process, helping policyholders gather documentation, and answering any questions they may have.

It's also important for adjusters to be flexible and adaptable in these situations. Natural disasters can often cause disruptions and delays, and it's important for adjusters to be able to adjust their schedules and processes as needed in order to effectively assist policyholders.

Another difficult situation that adjusters may encounter is dealing with policyholders who have experienced significant losses. This can be emotionally challenging for both the policyholder and the adjuster, and it's important to approach these situations with empathy and sensitivity.

One way to handle these situations is to provide support and resources to the policyholder. This can include referrals to grief counseling or financial advisors, as well as providing information on available support services. It's also important for adjusters to be patient and understanding when working with policyholders who have experienced significant losses. These policyholders may be dealing with a range of emotions, and it's important to provide a supportive and compassionate environment as they navigate the claims process.

In situations where a policyholder is unhappy with the settlement offer, it's important for adjusters to be able to communicate effectively and address any concerns that the policyholder may have. This can involve explaining the reasoning behind the offer and discussing any options that may be available to the policyholder. It's also important for adjusters to be open to negotiation and to be willing to consider alternative solutions.

As an adjuster, it is not uncommon to encounter difficult situations on a regular basis. These situations can range from dealing with upset and angry policyholders as discussed, to negotiating with resistant insurance companies, to handling complex and high-stakes claims. No matter the specific challenge, it is important for adjusters to have strategies in place to effectively handle difficult situations and find practical solutions.

One common difficult situation that adjusters face is dealing with upset and angry policyholders. This can occur for a variety of reasons, such as the policyholder feeling that their claim is not being handled properly, or that the payout they receive is not sufficient. In these situations, it is important for adjusters to remain calm and professional, and to focus on finding a resolution that will satisfy the policyholder.

One practical step that adjusters can take in these situations is to listen carefully to the policyholder's concerns and address them directly. This may involve explaining the claims process and the reasoning behind certain decisions, or negotiating with the insurance company to try and increase the payout. It is also important for adjusters to be empathetic and understanding, and to offer support and assistance throughout the claims process.

Another difficult situation that adjusters may encounter is negotiating with resistant insurance companies. This can occur when the insurance company is unwilling to pay out on a claim, or when they are offering a payout that is significantly lower than what the policyholder is expecting. In these situations, it is important for adjusters to be assertive and persistent, and to negotiate for the best possible outcome for the policyholder.

One practical step that adjusters can take in these situations is to thoroughly review the policy and the circumstances surrounding the claim, and to use this information to build a strong case for why the claim should be paid out. This may involve gathering evidence and documentation, such as photographs, reports, and expert opinions, to support the policyholder's case. It may also involve working with legal counsel to ensure that the policyholder's rights are being protected.

Another practical step that adjusters can take in these situations is to communicate clearly and effectively with the insurance company, and to be willing to compromise and negotiate in order to reach a resolution. This may involve offering alternative solutions or compromising on certain aspects of the claim in order to reach an agreement.

One final difficult situation that adjusters may encounter is handling complex and high-stakes claims. These claims may involve large sums of money, or may have significant legal or regulatory implications. In these situations, it is important for adjusters to be thorough and meticulous, and to follow all appropriate procedures and protocols in order to ensure that the claim is handled correctly.

One practical step that adjusters can take in these situations is to seek out additional resources and expertise as needed. This may involve consulting with legal counsel, working with specialized experts, or seeking out guidance from other adjusters or industry professionals. It is also important for adjusters to keep detailed records and documentation, and to be prepared to present their findings and recommendations in a clear and concise manner.

Another practical step that adjusters can take in these situations is to be proactive and proactive in managing the claim. This may involve setting clear goals and timelines, and regularly communicating with all relevant parties to ensure that the claim is moving forward smoothly. It may also involve taking steps to minimize potential delays or complications, such as by anticipating and addressing potential issues or challenges before they arise.

In conclusion, adjusters often face a variety of difficult situations in the course of their work. These can range from dealing with upset and angry policyholders, to negotiating with resistant insurance companies, to handling complex and high-stakes claims. In order to effectively handle these challenges, it is important for adjusters to have strategies.

Chapter 16

SELF-CARE

Self-care is an essential aspect of life, especially for those who work in demanding and stressful fields like insurance adjusting. Being an adjuster can be physically and emotionally draining, as you are constantly interacting with clients, processing complex claims, and working long hours. It's important to prioritize self-care in order to maintain your physical and mental health, as well as your overall well-being.

Here are some practical steps you can take to prioritize self-care as an adjuster:

1. Set boundaries: It's important to set boundaries around your work and personal life to ensure that you have time for self-care. This might involve setting specific hours for work, delegating tasks to coworkers, and saying no to unreasonable requests.

2. Take breaks: It's essential to take breaks throughout the

day to rest and recharge. This could be as simple as stepping away from your desk for a few minutes to take a walk or stretch, or taking a longer break to eat lunch or go for a walk.

3. Exercise regularly: Exercise is an important aspect of self-care as it helps to reduce stress and improve overall physical and mental health. Find an activity that you enjoy, such as running, yoga, or weight lifting, and make time to engage in it regularly.

4. Practice good sleep hygiene: Getting enough sleep is crucial for maintaining physical and mental health. This includes establishing a consistent sleep schedule, avoiding screens before bed, and creating a comfortable sleep environment.

5. Eat a healthy diet: A well-balanced diet can help to boost your energy levels and improve your overall well-being. Make sure to include plenty of fruits, vegetables, and whole grains in your diet, and avoid processed and sugary foods.

6. Connect with others: It's important to have a support system to help you through the stresses of your job. Make time to connect with friends and family regularly, and consider joining a support group or finding a therapist to talk to.

7. Take time off: It's important to take regular vacations and time off work to rest and recharge. Plan a trip, or simply take a few days off to relax and recharge.

8. Practice mindfulness: Mindfulness involves being present in the moment and focusing on your thoughts and feelings without judgment. This can help to reduce stress

and improve overall well-being. Consider incorporating mindfulness practices into your daily routine, such as meditation or journaling.

9. Engage in self-care activities: Self-care activities are things that you do specifically for your own well-being, such as taking a bubble bath or getting a massage. Make time for these activities regularly to help you relax and recharge.

10. Seek help when needed: If you're feeling overwhelmed or struggling with your mental health, it's important to seek help. Talk to a trusted friend, family member, or therapist, or consider seeking professional treatment.

By incorporating these self-care practices into your daily routine, you can help to reduce stress and improve your overall well-being. Remember to be kind to yourself and take the time you need to rest and recharge. Your physical and mental health are essential to your overall well-being, and by prioritizing self-care, you can better handle the demands of your job as an adjuster.

Self-Development: Questions Adjusters Can ask Themselves to Regain Control

Adjusters should ask themselves the following questions when they feel themselves losing control of the conversation with the insured:

1. What is the root cause of my discomfort or frustration in this conversation?

2. How can I refocus the conversation on the facts and the policy at hand?

3. Am I listening actively and allowing the insured to fully express their concerns or grievances?

4. Am I maintaining a professional and empathetic tone, or am I allowing my emotions to influence the conversation?

5. How can I calmly and effectively address any confrontational or aggressive behavior from the insured?

6. Can I involve a supervisor or mediator to help diffuse the situation if necessary?

7. Am I maintaining a clear and objective perspective, or am I becoming too personally invested in the outcome of the conversation?

Self-Development: Questions Adjusters Can ask Themselves to When Building Relationships

1. What are the client's needs and goals for their insurance coverage? How can I best support them in meeting those goals?

2. How can I communicate effectively with the client to ensure they understand their coverage and the claims process?

3. What expectations does the client have of me as their adjuster? How can I meet or exceed those expectations?

4. How can I build trust with the client through my actions and communication?

5. How can I work effectively with my manager and other team members to support the client and resolve their claims efficiently?

6. How can I continue to educate myself and stay up-to-date on industry best practices and regulations to better serve the client?

7. How can I build positive relationships with other professionals in the industry, such as contractors and attorneys, to better serve the client's needs?

Self-Development: Questions Adjusters Can ask Themselves for Self-care

1. Have I been feeling overwhelmed or stressed lately?

2. Have I been neglecting my physical or emotional well-being?

3. Have I been skipping meals, exercising, or sleeping less than usual?

4. Have I been experiencing a negative impact on my relationships or work performance due to my lack of self-care?

5. Have I been struggling to find time or motivation to prioritize my own needs?

6. Am I consistently feeling burnt out or drained?

7. Have I been relying on unhealthy coping mechanisms to deal with stress?

In conclusion, self-care is crucial for insurance adjusters to practice in order to maintain their physical and mental health while working in a demanding and stressful field. It is important to set boundaries, prioritize time for relaxation and self-care activities,

EPILOGUE

In the fast-paced and often high-stress world of insurance adjusting, the ability to communicate effectively, work well with others, and manage our time and emotions can be the key to thriving. As adjusters, it is not only important to have a strong foundation of technical knowledge and expertise, but it is also crucial to possess a set of soft skills that can help you thrive in your profession. These skills, often referred to as interpersonal or people skills, involve the ability to communicate effectively, build relationships, and handle difficult situations with tact and diplomacy. In this epilogue, we will explore some key soft skills that can help you succeed as an adjuster and how to develop them.

Communication skills are essential for adjusters, as you will be interacting with a variety of people on a daily basis, including policyholders, claimants, insurance company representatives, and colleagues. It is important to be able to clearly and accurately convey information, as well as actively listen and understand the perspectives of others. Whether we are speaking with clients, colleagues, or superiors, the ability to convey our thoughts and ideas in a clear and concise manner is essential. This includes not just the words we use, but also our body language and tone of voice.

Effective communication also involves active listening. This means really paying attention to what others are saying, rather than just waiting for our turn to speak. It's important to listen actively not just to understand what others are saying, but also to build trust and rapport. Building relationships can help you gather important information and resources, as well as facilitate a smooth claims process. To improve your relationship-building skills, try to be approachable and friendly, show empathy and understanding towards others, and be willing to listen to their needs and concerns.

In addition to communication and relationship-building skills, it is important for adjusters to have the ability to handle difficult situations with tact and diplomacy. This may involve handling difficult claimants, mediating disputes, or navigating complex legal issues. To develop these skills, it can be helpful to practice conflict resolution techniques, such as active listening, compromise, and seeking win-win solutions. It is also important to remain calm and level-headed in challenging situations, and to seek guidance and support from colleagues or superiors when needed.

Other important soft skills for adjusters include problem-solving abilities, adaptability, and a strong work ethic. To improve your problem-solving skills, try to approach challenges with a logical and systematic mindset, and seek out resources and ideas from others. Being adaptable and flexible can also be helpful, as the claims process can often involve unexpected challenges and changing circumstances. Finally, having a strong work ethic and a dedication to quality can help you stand out as a reliable and dependable adjuster.

Effective time management is another crucial soft skill for adjusters. In a field where deadlines are often tight and the workload can be overwhelming, the ability to prioritize tasks and manage our time effectively is essential. This includes setting clear goals and objectives, creating a schedule and sticking to it, and being able to adapt to changing circumstances.

Emotional intelligence is also important for adjusters. This includes being able to manage our own emotions, as well as being able to understand and respond to the emotions of others. In a field where we often deal with clients who are upset or distressed, the ability to remain calm and empathetic is essential.

Finally, the ability to adapt and be flexible is another important soft skill for adjusters. With constant changes in the insurance industry and a never-ending stream of new challenges and opportunities, the ability to adapt and be flexible is key to our success.

Overall, it's clear that soft skills are an essential part of thriving as an adjuster. While technical knowledge and expertise are certainly important, it's the ability to communicate effectively, work well with others, manage our time and emotions, and adapt and be flexible that often makes the biggest difference in our success. By continuing to develop and hone these skills, we can ensure that we continue to thrive in the fast-paced and ever-changing world of insurance adjusting.

Soft skills are an integral part of a thriving adjuster's toolkit. By developing your communication, relationship-building, and conflict resolution skills, as well as your problem-solving abilities, adaptability, and work ethic, you can set yourself up for success in your profession. Remember to continually seek out opportunities to learn and improve, and seek guidance from colleagues and superiors when needed. With a strong foundation of both technical knowledge and soft skills, you can thrive as an adjuster and make a meaningful impact in your profession.

Self-care is a term that is often used in the context of personal well-being and self-improvement. However, it is equally important for those who work in the field of insurance adjusting. Adjusters play a crucial role in the insurance industry, as they are responsible for evaluating and settling insurance claims. This can be a stressful and demanding job, as adjusters often have to deal with difficult clients, navigate complex legal and regulatory issues, and handle sensitive personal information.

As a result, self-care is essential for adjusters to maintain their physical, emotional, and mental health. Without proper self-care, adjusters may be more prone to burnout, which can lead to a decrease in productivity, an increase in absenteeism, and even long-term health problems.

One of the most important aspects of self-care for adjusters is taking care of their physical health. This includes getting enough sleep, eating a healthy diet, and exercising regularly. Adjusters often work long hours, and it can be tempting to neglect self-care in the face of tight deadlines and demanding clients. However, taking care of one's physical health is essential for maintaining energy and focus, and for avoiding problems such as weight gain, high blood pressure, and other health issues.

Another important aspect of self-care for adjusters is managing their stress levels. Adjusters often deal with high levels of stress, whether it is due to difficult clients, complex legal issues, or a heavy workload. Stress can have negative effects on both physical and mental health, and it is important for adjusters to find ways to manage and reduce their stress levels. This can include practicing relaxation techniques such as meditation or yoga, taking regular breaks, and setting boundaries around work.

One way that adjusters can practice self-care is by setting aside time for themselves. This can include activities such as taking a walk, reading a book, or spending time with friends and family. Adjusters should also make sure to take regular vacations and breaks from work to recharge and rejuvenate.

In addition to taking care of their physical and emotional well-being, it is also important for adjusters to prioritize their mental health. This includes practicing self-care activities such as journaling, seeking therapy or counseling when needed, and finding healthy ways to cope with stress and negative emotions.

Self-care is not just about taking care of oneself in the short-term, but also about building long-term resilience and sustainability. By practicing self-care on a regular basis, adjusters can better manage their stress levels, improve their productivity, and ultimately lead happier and healthier lives.

It is also important for adjusters to remember that self-care is not selfish. By taking care of themselves, adjusters can better serve their clients and colleagues, and contribute to a positive work environment.

In conclusion, self-care is essential for adjusters to maintain their physical, emotional, and mental health. By prioritizing self-care, adjusters can better manage their stress levels, improve their productivity, and lead happier and healthier lives. Ultimately, self-care is an investment in one's overall well-being and long-term sustainability in the demanding field of insurance adjusting.

Made in the USA
Columbia, SC
19 February 2025